AMERICA'S
DISENFRANCHISED

McCourtney Institute for Democracy

The Pennsylvania State University's McCourtney Institute for Democracy (http://democracyinstitute.la.psu.edu) was founded in 2012 as an interdisciplinary center for research, teaching, and outreach on democracy. The institute coordinates innovative programs and projects in collaboration with the Center for American Political Responsiveness and the Center for Democratic Deliberation.

Laurence and Lynne Brown Democracy Medal

The Laurence and Lynne Brown Democracy Medal recognizes outstanding individuals, groups, and organizations that produce exceptional innovations to further democracy in the United States or around the world. In even-numbered years, the medal spotlights practical innovations, such as new institutions, laws, technologies, or movements that advance the cause of democracy. Awards given in odd-numbered years highlight advances in democratic theory that enrich philosophical conceptions of democracy or empirical models of democratic behavior, institutions, or systems.

AMERICA'S DISENFRANCHISED

WHY RESTORING THEIR VOTE CAN SAVE THE SOUL OF OUR DEMOCRACY

DESMOND MEADE

CORNELL UNIVERSITY PRESS

Ithaca and London

Thanks to generous funding from the McCourtney Institute for Democracy at Pennsylvania State University, the ebook editions of this book are available as open access volumes through the Cornell Open initiative.

First published 2021 by Cornell University Press

Library of Congress Cataloging-in-Publication Data
Library of Congress Control Number: 2021943569

ISBN: 978-1-5017-6374-8 (paperback)
ISBN: 978-1-5017-6375-5 (ebook)
ISBN: 978-1-5017-6376-2 (pdf)

Contents

Introduction   1

Jim Crow at the Ballot Box   11

The Campaign   17

Lessons Learned from Second Chances Campaign   39

Old Habits Are Hard to Break   46

Conclusion   63

Notes   69

About the Author   73

AMERICA'S
DISENFRANCHISED

Introduction

Like a lot of people, I spent very little time contemplating the connection between law, criminal justice, and democracy. It wasn't until I had a direct experience of punishment for breaking the law and becoming an advocate for change—ultimately leading a campaign for constitutional reform in Florida—that I was able to thread the needle between all three. Civic, political, and social life in the United States is governed by statutes that most of us seldom consider unless we are directly confronted by their consequences for ourselves and others. Yet I also believe that the infiltration of partisanship in all of these areas threatens the democracy we aspire to have.

As I learned firsthand from my experience with crime and punishment (a story I'll share later in this essay), sometimes the consequences of conviction are far reaching, with implications beyond the specific statute in question. Until recently, in my home state of Florida, anyone who was incarcerated for a felony would not only be required to serve time, pay fines, and compensate the victims, but would then face the permanent loss of voting rights. That person could never again participate in elections.

The punitive law that stripped *returning citizens*—people who are convicted of crimes, serve time, and then resume regular life and activities after paying their debts—of their vote, disenfranchising millions of Floridians over the decades, fundamentally alters the politics of our state and, arguably, the nation. Right now, in the United States of America, over six million people have paid their debts to society for past mistakes, yet they cannot vote.

In 2018, my organization, the Florida Rights Restoration Coalition, led a dark-horse campaign to change the law in Florida by amending our state constitution at the ballot box. This essay will look at why it was necessary, how we overcame partisanship to win a landslide victory, and how its lessons can help save American democracy.

The Impact of Law and Criminal Justice

The definition of a *felony* varies widely from state to state. In Florida, a felony is defined as any crime for which the punishment can exceed a year of imprisonment. Felonies in Florida cover a wide range of illegal behaviors.

Additionally, the state also has a low threshold for felony conviction when it comes to some crimes. For years, for instance, Florida's felony theft threshold was just $300—much lower than neighboring states like Georgia or South Carolina which classify comparable thefts as misdemeanors. All this means that in Florida felony convictions are comparatively quite common.

In 2010, the last year for which comprehensive data is available, the average national rate of felony conviction was at 8.11 percent of the voting-age population. The rate was almost double that in Florida, at just over 15 percent. Black and Brown Floridians are disproportionately affected in large part because we are more likely to be arrested for drug offenses. And because a felony conviction triggers a loss of civil rights, including the right to vote, one in five Black Floridians were left unable to participate in any election.[1] The vast majority of these people were not, in fact, behind bars. Like myself, they were returning citizens—people who paid their debts, served their time, and were discharged to resume life in the community. And since our exclusion from voting took away our ability to choose the decision-makers who determine key policies that shape incarceration and reentry, we were also left without the means to address these problems.

Returning citizens face a range of obstacles in reentering communities, including barriers to employment, housing, health care, and basic social services.[2] For example, notwithstanding my contribution to restoring voting rights to returning citizens, the many accolades and awards I received for my leadership, and the material success that accompanies the executive directorship of a major organization, my history of felony conviction still hurts many aspects of my life, just as it does for millions of others who share this experience. I graduated from law school, but am prohibited from taking the Florida bar exam or actually practicing law. I have been named on the "*Time* 100 Most Influential People" list, but because of the felony on my record, I still can't get approval for a lease.[3] For returning citizens like me, it's a long and winding road not just to equal rights, but to fairness and redemption. That's why my organization, the Florida Rights Restoration Coalition, ultimately organized returning citizens and their families for the long haul.

Throughout my early advocacy days, I spent a considerable amount of time engaged in "get out the vote" and voter registration efforts. I would often encounter people whose response to my effort would be, "I don't have time to waste on that"; "My vote doesn't count"; or, "Even if I vote, it doesn't matter who gets in office; we're still screwed!" I was always taught to not debate with people when they refuse to engage. My supervisor always told me to keep it moving; primarily because I needed to have a certain amount of engagements on a daily basis. I needed to "make the numbers," or meet the quota. When I first started, I used to adhere to that guidance, but eventually I became too curious to continue to ignore these frequent responses. I just had to know what it was that caused people to feel so apathetic about voting; what was making people lose hope in a democracy that was supposed to be for them. So I broke the rule. One day after I was given the typical response, I started to walk away, but I couldn't contain my curiosity any longer. I turned around and asked that person why they held that belief.

Almost immediately after starting the conversion, I discovered that this person couldn't even vote to begin with, having been barred from voting due to a prior felony conviction. This revelation took me back to a time after being released from prison. As I would be walking to some destination or another, someone would approach me and ask if I would like to register to vote, or if I would like to actually go and vote in a current election. These questions triggered an internal feeling of shame. It was a brutal reminder that I was not truly a part of my community; and telling someone about a past felony conviction or imprisonment is a badge of shame that I, like so many others, didn't care to share unless it was really necessary. I understood why someone could so easily respond with indifference. Nothing speaks more to citizenship than being able to vote; therefore, how can one feel like they are a part of society or a part of their community when they are being denied the franchise?

After that eye-opening conversation, I decided to figure out a way to quickly determine if someone's refusal to engage was because they didn't want to be bothered, or whether it was because they had been barred from voting. I developed an approach that allowed me, within a matter of seconds, to quickly identify who was the returning citizen. What I discovered was revelatory. The overwhelming number of people upset by my approach were returning citizens. It wasn't that a lot of people I encountered didn't care about participating in our democracy. It was that a lot of people I encountered believed that they could not.

I began to notice this narrative about voting not being important, or "our vote doesn't matter," was a story that was most prevalent among returning citizens. Its purpose was to mask the pain and embarrassment of exclusion. Worse, its effect reached into entire families and communities. The narrative is not exclusive to the encounter between activists and returning citizens. It also appears wherever and whenever there is a discussion about registering to vote or going to vote during an election. As a result, it is not only heard by activists, but also by family members, friends, and colleagues. Indeed, I also discovered that the impact of the loss of voting rights is not restricted to the returning citizen. Families and social networks also carry the burdens. I found that having someone in your life who is barred from voting can influence whether or not you vote, too: if the returning citizen is someone of influence within their circle of friends, family, or community—a not-uncommon situation—then whole groups of people who otherwise would be qualified to vote become uninterested in the process.

This deadening of voices is tragic. During the civil rights era, family played an important role in voting. When Mom and Dad went to the ballot box, the outing was a household affair. Everyone would get dressed in their "Sunday best" and head to the polling location, kids and all. Voting and civic engagement were a part of the family's dinner table discussions. Children heard early in life about the hard-won right to vote and how that hard work and sacrifice are honored when one votes. But when you strip Mom and Dad of the right to vote; when you use the mechanism of mass incarceration to erode the family structure; and when you utilize state-sanctioned tactics to discourage voter participation, those dinner table discussions become the exception rather than the norm. Those family trips to the polling location cease.

Case Background: Felony Disenfranchisement in Florida

Given the history, scale, and effects of felony disenfranchisement in Florida, the stakes of any effort to reverse the trend were incredibly high to start with. But the implications were compelling for our state and the country as a whole. A quick history of felony incarceration and disenfranchisement illustrates the point.

Despite falling incarceration rates over the last several years, the United States still has the highest rate in the world.[4]

It puts more people behind bars every year than any other nation. Moreover, even today in states like Virginia and Kentucky (and as recently as 2018 in Florida and 2020 in Iowa), state-level systems effectively erase these individuals from our democracy by denying them the right to vote. The United States is not the only place where incarcerated people face punitive voting prohibitions, but it is an outlier in its failure to automatically restore those voting rights once a person's sentences are complete and their debts are paid. We are the only postindustrial country where those with felony records can be permanently disenfranchised.

In a nation where more people are convicted and incarcerated for felonies than anywhere in the world, the disenfranchisement of people with felony convictions has tremendous implications for democracy. Florida is ground zero for those implications. It's the nation's biggest and highest-profile "battleground" state, an epicenter of demographic shifts in the voting-age population and home to a litany of razor-thin election victories. And while Florida was not alone in denying incarcerated people their democratic voice, the state has been unique for the sheer volume of its disenfranchised people. Nationwide in 2016, over 4.7 million of the 6.1 million people who were disenfranchised were not incarcerated but also not legally permitted to vote. Before passage of Amendment 4, Florida accounted for nearly 30 percent of that national total. Remember that the majority of disenfranchised people are actually not behind bars, but returning citizens like myself. They are out of jail or prison and living in communities where they typically work, pay taxes, abide by the law, and live normally—but for all that, they continue to be excluded from the democratic process and face a host of additional barriers to employment, housing, and resources.

Meanwhile, according to the Prison Policy Institute, Florida's rate of incarceration still exceeds both the US national average and rates in any country.[5] Today, 176,000 Floridians are locked up in various facilities. Black and Brown people are overrepresented in Florida prisons and jails. Black felons are incarcerated at over three times the rate of White felons; Hispanics at twice the rate. Black Floridians are not the only people affected by voter disenfranchisement, but it is the ethnic group that feels it the most.

These numbers make the disenfranchisement of felons not just a voting-rights issue, but a civil rights battle. And in the case of Florida, that battle stretches back 150 years. The state's first constitution stripped people convicted of felonies of their right to vote permanently, and as the years progressed, that law remained among the most restrictive in the nation. It is well documented that the impetus behind felon disenfranchisement laws in the South rested on the back of racism, and I believe that racism is a real poison to the democracy we aspire to live in. As we would eventually prove in our campaign to reverse some of these injustices, the key to victory was to find a way past racism and connect returning citizens as Americans, friends, brothers, pastors, mothers, and colleagues, restoring our democracy from the community upward.

But it would not be an easy argument to make, not at first. To understand why, we have to understand a little bit of history.

Jim Crow at the Ballot Box

There was a time when the United States believed that only wealthy landowners should have a say in our democracy. Despite the assertion in the Declaration of Independence that all men were created equal, enslaved people were once considered only "property." But, over time, beginning with the 14th Amendment of the US Constitution, we saw an evolution that reflected the sentiment that our democracy should be more inclusive and live up to its founding ideals.

The implications of the Emancipation Proclamation, the Union victory over the secessionist Southern states, and the subsequent changes to the United States Constitution (the so-called Civil War amendments) were understandably a cultural shock to the slave owners and like-minded White Americans of the day. After all, slave owners believed with conviction that their slaves were inferior beings, undeserving of human dignity. And then they were suddenly being told that their slaves are people with rights; and the victors came into their states to enforce this new understanding. While this radical new view was still sinking in, these formerly enslaved people were already exercising their newfound rights by becoming active participants in the democratic process. They were voting and even getting elected to office. How alarming it must have been for the former slave owner to recognize the new state representative or senator as the son of the man he just recently whipped so brutally, or the son of the woman he once raped. As it's often said, "It ain't fun when the rabbit got the gun!"

In the minds of former slave owners, something had to be done, once their Southern states again had the power to act. In order to "right the wrongs" of the federal government's intrusion into the Southern social order, Jim Crow laws proliferated. The laws reestablished Black Americans as second-class citizens in Southern society, and through laws, violence, manipulation, and unfair implementation of various requirements, they also effectively eliminated Black enfranchisement.

But the cornerstone for the exceptional (and dubious) status of the United States as the only nation in the world where felons can be permanently stripped of their voting rights came from an unlikely source: the 14th Amendment of the United States Constitution itself, the very amendment that enfranchised former slaves.

Section 2 of the 14th Amendment contains a key provision: its freedoms extended to all citizens "except for [those guilty of] participation in rebellion, or other crime." Here is the foundation for the implementation of felon disenfranchisement policies at the state level. Again, Florida's first constitution reads, "The General Assembly shall have the power to exclude from . . . suffrage, all persons convicted of bribery, perjury, forgery, or other high crime, or misdemeanor." The 14th Amendment gave Florida's ruling elite all the justification they needed to continue this policy, even as Jim Crow made a farce of the equality the Amendment was meant to ensure. Even embedded in the bedrock of our freedom was a toehold for Jim Crow—it seemed inescapable, and eventually, inescapably partisan; whether it was the Dixiecrats or eventual Republicans, Jim Crow was a legal way to minimize potential negative electoral impact on one's political party.

In short, a century and a half later, when we at the Florida Rights Restoration Coalition began our campaign for change, we were facing a wall of history. The one exception was the Florida Correction Reform Act of 1974 which, for a flicker in time, had automatically restored civil rights, including voting rights, once an individual was released from prison or discharged from parole or probation. But the following year, the Florida Supreme Court had issued an advisory opinion that found the act to be unconstitutional because the state's constitution at the time gave the power of clemency exclusively to the governor and cabinet. Until 2018, and our attempt to remedy this antiquated law, there was only one way for disenfranchised people to get their voting rights back: they had to ask the state governor to restore those rights on a case-by-case basis through an opaque clemency process that took years and created tremendous hurdles. Even more important, the decision was arbitrary. When asked about what it takes to have voting rights restored, Florida governor Rick Scott replied: "There is no standard. We can do whatever we want."[6] And that is exactly what he did. Governor Scott used the arbitrariness associated with his powers to shift what should have been the apolitical matter of granting clemency into a politicized one.

Governor Scott restored voting rights for fewer Black Floridians than any of the governors before him, Republican or Democrat, going back at least fifty years. To put this into perspective, in the four years of Governor Jeb Bush's administration, over 75,000 people were able to get their civil rights restored. In the four years of Governor Charlie Crist's administration, over 155,000 people were able to get their civil rights restored. But in the eight years of Governor Scott's administration, fewer than 5,000 of the 20,000 petitioners were successfully re-enfranchised. Scott also restored voting rights to a higher percentage of Republican voters and lower percentage of Democrats than any of his predecessors of either party since 1971. An analysis from the *Palm Beach Post* revealed that not only did Governor Scott's policy result in very few Floridians regaining voting rights, but the implementation of the policy favored White and Republican Floridians over Black and Brown voters. Although Blacks and Hispanics are incarcerated at much higher rates than Whites and comprise a much larger share of disenfranchised voters in the state, the Scott administration restored voting rights for twice as many Whites as Blacks during his years as governor.

I started to realize that even though the decision to restore civil rights should not have been a political one, it was left in the hands of politicians—people who needed to be voted into office. So, it was going to be difficult to get any governor, Republican or Democrat, to ignore the political ramifications of revising the clemency policy. In addition to the considerations of politicians, I also noticed the political consideration of voters. When faced with a purely political perspective on the restoration of voting rights, embedded in a conventional, biased assumption that it was mostly African Americans who were disenfranchised, the response was predictably grounded in a partisan calculus. Most Blacks vote Democratic. Therefore, when the question of re-enfranchisement came up, the Democrats were mainly for it, and the Republicans were mainly against it. I am not saying that this was true for everyone, but it was prevalent in the thousands of face-to-face discussions I've had throughout the state. Restoring voting rights to people with previous felony convictions was either a way to turn Florida "blue" (if you were talking to a

Democrat) or a dastardly attempt by liberals to gain votes (if you were talking to a Republican).

Lost in those competing motivations was a greater consideration of simple fairness. Weed away the centuries of bias and the political realities associated with an evenly divided populace, and there were real people affected by the law. Real shame, embarrassment, and disaffection were living in the minds of American citizens who had repaid their debts to society, as well as in the minds of those who loved and supported them.

Disenfranchisement has a personal impact felt by real people, and it distorts what we want democracy to look like. Are we looking for a society in which the only outcome that matters is that our side wins? Or do we want a society that recognizes that democracy works better when we accept differing opinions, perspectives, and ideals, and affirm that everyone has the right to participate? I believe that a true champion of democracy should be motivated to protect and restore voting rights regardless of how the beneficiaries might vote. Advocacy for voting rights should be just as fervent for the people who don't agree with me as it is for those that do—and when I began a journey of hundreds of thousands of miles to talk to people all over Florida about returning citizens' need for a voice, that message resonated. It also led to the first successful constitutional challenge to that wall of historical injustice, creating the first cracks.

The Campaign

Whether we realize it or not, denying formerly incarcerated people in Florida the right to vote has affected everyone in this nation. Not just because of the effect it has on the individual returning citizen or voter, but also because it justifies and encourages the practice of excluding American citizens from engaging in the most telling act of citizenship. We saw this play out in the 2000 Bush-versus-Gore election contest. The felon disenfranchisement policy was used as a pretext to remove 12,000 eligible voters in an election decided by fewer than 550 votes. The 2000 election heightened the role that voter suppression tactics can play; particularly in close elections, and as Ari Berman reported in *The Nation*, "empowered a new generation of voting rights critics, who hyped the threat of voter fraud in order to restrict access to the ballot, and remade a Supreme Court that would eventually gut the centerpiece of the VRA."[7] Eliminating felon disenfranchisement is one of the first steps toward creating the kind of democracy that works for everyone in this country. It sets a bar for inclusiveness. If we recognize that access to the ballot box should be granted even to the citizens who may have committed a crime, then it would be unacceptable to deny access to anyone else. The more inclusive the access, the more vibrant the democracy, and the more vibrant the democracy, the better it is for everyone.

Prior to our Amendment 4 campaign, Florida was one of only a handful of states that permanently disfranchised people with felony convictions. Alongside states such as Kentucky, Virginia, and (formerly) Iowa, Florida distinguished itself primarily due to the sheer volume of disenfranchised citizens. As I have noted, at its height, 1.68 million people could not vote due to a previous felony conviction. Consequently, Florida, by itself, accounted for approximately one-quarter of the nation's disenfranchised adults. There were more of them here, in my state, than the population of over fourteen other US states and territories, and over forty countries in the world. In essence, not letting returning citizens vote in Florida is like denying the right to vote to the entire population of Maine, Rhode Island, Alaska, or Wyoming.

The fact that Florida is also a key swing state in presidential elections expands the impact of felon disenfranchisement beyond our state borders. We've seen several presidential elections in the last twenty years determined by the outcome of races here, and the difference in those races is almost always narrow, such as the 550 votes in the 2000 election. To know that there were times when the fate of our country hung in the balance in a state in which over one million citizens were denied the opportunity to cast a ballot spoke to a failing of our democracy, but also of an opportunity to empower and infuse a significant base of citizens into the messy but exciting world of democratic politics.

My Story

Most people know that my involvement in the restoration of voting rights in Florida originated in my own experience as a returning citizen. This journey is related at greater length in my book, *Let My People Vote: My Battle to Restore the Civil Rights of Returning Citizens*, but here's the short version: from 2001 to 2004, I served a sentence in a Florida state prison, experiencing firsthand the plight of incarceration and then the persistent stigma, penalties, and discrimination that comes with life after release.

Reentry isn't easy. I had no plan and few possibilities. Like most other returning citizens, my first concern wasn't voting. It was basic survival: Where was I going to live? How could I get a job? How was I going to continue recovery and treatment for the addiction that landed me behind bars to begin with? I was alienated from my family, had no income, and soon became homeless again. In a cycle I had experienced before, I descended back into drug dependency and was close to giving up hope on myself and on life. In fact, in August 2005, I found myself on the railroad tracks, having decided that suicide was the only escape from the torment I was experiencing.

But the train never came. Having failed at suicide, I crossed the tracks, and somehow that moment put me in motion in a new direction. Ironically, the same addiction that led me to prison eventually also led me to advocacy. I enrolled in a drug rehabilitation program and, after I completed the program, I moved into a homeless shelter. Then, in January 2006, I enrolled in community college. The goal was just to stay as busy as possible with structured activity in order to continue my recovery process, and at the same time gain some skills to make a living. I chose to enroll in paralegal studies—a natural direction since I had worked on my own case while incarcerated, petitioning the court to file a belated appeal. I had been successful and then went on to help others with their legal paperwork as well.

For me, those encounters with the law eventually translated into a passion to reform the Constitution, but achieving that goal actually prompted a much larger transformation. Over the years, I became a student of the law and then a law school graduate. I started as an activist looking to address my own issue, but I became an organizer across key constituencies and eventually the face of a movement that would one day outline a comprehensive vision for returning citizens and their communities.

Embracing the law in a more systematic way helped me shift focus from my own problems and history to a bigger perspective that expanded my sense of purpose. To satisfy that end, I first got involved with the Homeless/Formerly Homeless Forum, a community organization focused on combating homelessness. It was through this group that I first came to understand that returning citizens could not vote in Florida and that the process of getting voting rights back was a long and cumbersome one—fraught with barriers and unlikely to yield results.

In August 2008, I attended a convening of the Florida Rights Restoration Coalition (FRRC). At that time, the FRRC was a loose collection of allies and advocates—little more than a listserv. I didn't know anyone at the meeting except other homelessness advocates, but the meeting had a tremendous impact on me. I gained an understanding of the effect that my conviction had on my right to vote, and I was introduced to the history of felon disenfranchisement and its disproportionate impact on African Americans. When I started fully engaging in the monthly conference calls with the FRRC, I realized the breadth of felon disenfranchisement's impact on the country. All of a sudden, I was struck with an epiphany that made me understand my real purpose in life: to inspire others with hope for change. At that

moment, I fully embraced service and stepped up my participation in the FRRC's regular conference calls.

In another sign of divine providence, I was nominated
by a total stranger to become the next steering committee
secretary. Even though I did not have any experience and
I definitely did not type well, I accepted a job whose duties
included taking copious notes during the meetings and pre-
paring meeting minutes for the subsequent meetings. Those
calls featured legal experts from the NAACP (National
Association for the Advancement of Colored People), the
Advancement Project, the Brennan Center for Justice, the
Sentencing Project, and the ACLU (American Civil Liberties
Union), among others, often discussing the many aspects of
the felony disenfranchisement issue. I learned a lot about the
law and the issue through this work. For one thing, efforts
to restore voting rights to Florida's disenfranchised, formerly incarcerated people were not new. In 2000, in *Johnson
v. Bush*, legal advocates at the Brennan Center led an effort
representing more than 600,000 Floridians to challenge the
state's constitutional provision that permanently disenfranchised people.[8] They had not been successful, but advocates
were also not deterred.

Recall that in Florida the only way to restore a person's
right to vote once it has been stripped away was as a favor
granted by the governor. The only viable way to change that
policy was by constitutional amendment. In 2003 there had
been a previous citizen-led ballot measure effort to change

the Florida Constitution regarding voting rights for returning citizens, but the petition had gathered only a few hundred signatures, well short of what was needed. Legal experts on the monthly FRRC calls continued to strategize, however, looking at recent developments from other states that might inform our local efforts. In particular, we looked at whether a state allowed constitutional amendment initiatives, and if not, we looked at a state's legislative and executive branches' attitudes toward felon disenfranchisement. In Virginia, which was one of the four states that permanently disenfranchised its citizens who had been convicted of a felony, there was no option to engage in a ballot initiative, but there had been a concentrated grassroots effort to convince the state's governors over the years to use their executive powers to address the issue. We were even able to use in our message some of the language that Virginia's conservative attorney general and governor used in supporting the restoration of civil rights.

We discussed how Florida voters could put something on the ballot if they gathered enough signatures and met all the criteria. Many of the experts of the day thought this tactic was too uphill, particularly after the passage of Jessica's Law in 2006, which galvanized public opinion against sex offenders and imposed more severe restrictions against people who commit these crimes.[9] Polling at that time showed low public support for enfranchising sex offenders.

FRRC allies focused their attention instead on legislative and executive advocacy. And they had some success.

In April 2007, Governor Charlie Crist persuaded the state's clemency board to accept revised rules that would automatically restore voting rights for people with some felony convictions.[10] According to Crist's administration, over 115,000 people gained voting rights through this reform. It was a move in the right direction but still left hundreds of thousands of returning citizens with no recourse.

I was among these petitioners, as a matter of fact. I had applied to have my voting rights restored in 2006, but as late as 2011, I was still waiting for my case to be considered. The policy had restored rights automatically for nonviolent offenses like mine, but the legislature reduced funding for the clemency board, creating a massive backlog of tens of thousands of us waiting to go through the process. When Governor Rick Scott was elected in 2008, replacing Crist, he instituted further restrictions, creating a five-to-seven-year wait before returning citizens could apply for voting rights restoration. Because of these new restrictions, I had to start all over again, forfeiting the two years I had already waited in the queue.

Caught in a system in which a handful of politicians had all the power to decide whether I should vote made me realize that partisan manipulation was flagrantly undermining the very bedrock of American democracy. I soon concluded that returning citizens had a better chance of changing the law than ever being served by it under the rigged system.

Consequently, I set about making a case to the experts that our odds of changing the constitution through a citizen petition were better than continued legislative or executive advocacy. In other words, I had to convince the experts that Florida's voters were more trustworthy than our politicians.

Advocacy to Organizing

At first the experts thought I was crazy. A citizen petition had been tried before and failed miserably, after all. In our discussions, I made the case that our own framing of the issue was undermining our cause. The prevailing narrative on felony disenfranchisement from progressives always elevated the disproportionate impact on voters of color—which the facts absolutely support.

From a strategic point of view, however, the exclusive focus on the Jim Crow legacy of felony disenfranchisement and disparate impact on Black Floridians framed this issue too narrowly to engage voters at the scale required to win a two-thirds vote. While felony disenfranchisement is undeniably a racial justice issue, it's not *just* a racial justice issue. In the 150 years since the Emancipation Proclamation, of course the law was undoubtedly meant to fetter Black voters' political power, but the impact of the law grew like a tumor over time, infecting masses of people well beyond that one demographic. The sheer scale of incarceration in Florida meant that hundreds of thousands of White Floridians had lost their rights, too, as did large numbers of Latino citizens.

As an amateur organizer, I relied primarily on my own experience as a returning citizen and on conveying a compelling vision of what rights restoration meant to me and my state. When I was first introduced to felon disenfranchisement at an FRRC convening in 2006, I had left the event with the conventional mindset that this issue was primarily an African American issue. For a couple of years afterward I always thought about felon disenfranchisement entirely through an African American lens, which as a result, led me to contemplate only on the impact of felon disenfranchisement on Black men. (Note: I do not mention Black women because at the time there was little to no research on the impact of felon disenfranchisement on Black women.) But my time on the road began to support the theory that this was too narrow a lens.

This reality opened up a new opportunity for building a much larger movement that spanned voting blocs, helping us build a coalition that could take back our collective rights. A successful strategy had to include all these groups of voters. It also needed an architecture to bring them together around larger shared values, not impact on any single group. Further, returning citizens would not be able to vote on restoration of their own voting rights, so it was essential that the voters in their families and communities—and ultimately the majority of Floridians—see a stake in this issue for themselves. Since that stake was not in fact their own legal rights, it must be a larger moral stake in supporting fairness, compassion, and human rights for all. Our campaign name, Second Chances, reflected this sensibility. Notably, the words "rights restoration" don't appear anywhere. Instead, our campaign slogan became "Say Yes to Second Chances," creating a message that animates empathy, fairness, and redemption.

Despite lingering doubts, the legal experts at the FRRC provided their help in crafting legal language for a ballot measure that would withstand scrutiny and stand up to potential challenges during the qualification process. Careful work spanning more than a year resulted in ballot language that we felt provided voters a clear understanding of the issue and the best opportunity for success. Before that language could be confirmed by the secretary of state, we had to gather enough citizen signatures to trigger (and pass) a legal review by the Florida Supreme Court.

In March 2017, we reached that milestone; volunteers had collected 68,314 signatures. Thanks to the careful work of legal allies, the court unanimously approved the language that ultimately appeared on the ballot:

This amendment restores the voting rights of Floridians with felony convictions after they complete all terms of their sentence including parole or probation. The amendment would not apply to those convicted of murder or sexual offenses, who would continue to be permanently barred from voting unless the Governor and Cabinet vote to restore their voting rights on a case by case basis.[11]

There was some controversy about excluding murder and sexual crimes from the ballot measure, but polling on the prospective measure suggested that including these offensives weakened public support significantly and created more opportunity for successful opposition to the measure. We therefore decided to create these exemptions in order to increase our chances for victory.

Testing a Theory of Nonpartisanship

Once the ballot language was accepted and certified, we were ready to start the process of qualifying the measure by gathering enough signatures to meet the criteria set by the Florida secretary of state. Although we cleared a hurdle in getting clear ballot language and certifying the language to appear, we still had an uphill battle to gather enough signatures to qualify the measure in time for the 2018 election.

Processes vary by state. In Florida, qualifying a ballot measure for a constitutional amendment requires gathering a number of signatures equal to 8 percent of the voters in the previous election. What is more, those signatures must come from at least half the state's congressional districts (at least fourteen of the twenty-seven). In 2018, we needed 760,200 signatures of verified registered voters to put rights restoration on the ballot.

While we were making steady progress and gaining momentum, the FRRC and our allies still lacked the funding to resource a full campaign. I did not let that deter me. I continued to travel around the state talking about restoring voting rights and enlisting my family, colleagues, and anyone I would meet on the road to do the same.

I traveled the state, speaking and listening. In Miami-Dade County, I met returning citizens who were Hispanic and of Haitian descent. As I started moving northward, I spoke mostly to returning citizens who were White. While I was accumulating all these miles on my car, I started appreciating the vast diversity of the returning citizen population. They were young, old, of all colors, and most interesting at the time, there were some who were conservative. This wasn't the demographic I was used to talking to; and I was surprised to discover African Americans who were also conservatives. These experiences made me reexamine how I was approaching the issue, and what emerged was an approach that did not look at felon disenfranchisement as an African American issue, but rather as an all-American issue.

This approach became a challenge at the beginning of the campaign because like me, my fellow advocates were so used to framing the campaign as an effort to right the racial wrongs of this country. The problem with this approach was that ballot initiatives are more difficult to pass in Florida than anywhere else in the country. While most states that allow their constitutions to be changed via an initiative require a simple majority of voter support to pass, in Florida we would need 60 percent of voters to approve our amendment. With such a high bar to pass, and taking into account the state's political and racial diversity, our efforts had to be about more than righting a racist wrong.

The other important and surprising problem was that while there was a disproportionate effect on the African American community, estimates actually showed us that this demographic only accounted for one-third of the disenfranchised population. At the time we were considering the campaign, we relied on the 2010 research conducted by Christopher Uggen and Sarah Shannon of the University of Minnesota, and Jeff Manza of New York University, which was published by the Sentencing Project in July 2012.[12] Their research estimated that 1.54 million Floridians could not vote because of their felony conviction. However, only about 500,000 were African Americans. While over twenty percent of the voting-age population of African Americans in Florida was disenfranchised, the reality that two-thirds of the total disenfranchised population belonged to other demographics created an opportunity to expand our initiative's support base.

We all have political or racial prisms that we use every day—we would be naive to believe that we don't—and these prisms trigger implicit biases. A person might therefore not be as committed to addressing a problem that is perceived to only be experienced by the "other." Thus, I was excited and hopeful that the key to our message might involve engaging people directly, through their own experiences and values. In other words, I no longer had to convince you to see the problem through my eyes. All I had to do was show you the issue through yours.

What I discovered in the process was that advocacy and organizing go hand-in-hand: the facts and figures alone did not persuade people that change was possible. Instead, I often inspired people to believe in the moral imperative to take action by laying out a vision for how our work together could change lives—not just the lives of the specific people who would regain the right to vote, but all our lives. I often shared my personal story, how my moment of epiphany on the train tracks inspired me to take action. I talked about my deep faith that Florida voters could overcome division and politics to do what's right. And indeed, I was surprised, but tremendously encouraged, to find as much support for restoring voting rights among White formerly incarcerated people as among Blacks and Latinos.

Lack of formal funding or infrastructure slowed our progress but ultimately it proved more a blessing than a curse in many ways. Doing much of the legwork myself increased my conviction about the kind of multiracial, statewide, movement-oriented effort we needed. The effort bolstered my faith that the change we sought was, in fact, possible. The volunteer energy we amassed and the benchmarks we reached because of that energy ultimately became the most compelling evidence of the viability of our campaign.

Soon, activists, clergy leaders, organizers from other movements and many others were actively talking about restoring Floridians' civil rights as a moral imperative. In the course of my travels, I met many allies who were to become central figures in the campaign. They included my future wife, Sheena, a labor and a community organizer who ultimately taught the rest of us the science of organizing. They also included Neil Volz, a White Republican returning citizen who co-led much of our campaign effort.

I met Neil in 2015 when I was giving a presentation at Gulf Coast University in Fort Myers. Neil had moved to Florida from Ohio after a felony conviction. He had worked as a legislative staffer for a prominent Republican leader, but after his felony he was doing outreach and janitorial work at a local church. In the course of my presentation, he asked me whether the campaign effort was nonpartisan. I immediately affirmed that this issue transcends politics. He agreed. Like me, Neil was rebuilding his life through public service—running a recovery program for people with addiction and support services for homeless people from his church.

The Second Chances campaign offered him a new mission, and he took it up immediately, quickly proving himself a key ally and effective organizer. Neil went back to his community and made the case for more conservatives to get involved. He posted information about meetings in local businesses like Gwendolyn's Cafe in downtown Fort Myers and showed up at Trump rallies with petitions to gather signatures to qualify the ballot measure. He organized training sessions at local libraries to train others to do the same, always staying away from partisan political pitches. Instead he emphasized the opportunity that attendees had to support and help their family members and neighbors, those people whom they loved and who deserved a second chance in rebuilding their lives.

Skeptics persisted. They said there was no way we could pass this kind of measure in Florida. But day after day, our own experience with voters from all walks of life bolstered our convictions. I received critical encouragement and support from Pastor Michael McBride, national leader of the Live Free Campaign. McBride agreed with me that directly affected people must lead the fight against mass incarceration and felony disenfranchisement, and he hired me on this team so that I could pursue building a campaign in Florida. With his support, our message attracted a massive network of allies and individuals who worked together in neighborhoods, churches, workplaces, and many other venues to gather over 1.1 million signatures to qualify the petition for the ballot. The effort took months and countless volunteers in every corner of the state.

As momentum for our cause increased, more and more allies stepped up to contribute support and capacity to the effort. Major donors also grew interested, contributing millions to individual organizations and to create the campaign. "Say Yes to Second Chances," the official ballot campaign to pass Amendment 4, launched in August 2017. We ultimately raised and spent a little over $22 million to pass the measure.

By the final stages of the campaign, Second Chances had brought together a diverse set of stakeholders across the political spectrum, including a wide range of congregations, the Florida Christian Coalition, Koch Industries, Families Against Mandatory Minimums, the Service Employees International Union, the NAACP, the League of Women Voters, and more. Momentum and energy was palpable on the ground. The campaign became a touchstone for national groups working on criminal justice, voting rights, and related issues, and our victory resounded in every corner of the country. As you can see from the list above, it also brought together unlikely allies that reflected a range of political views, which helped make our efforts less political. We'd touched a nerve, and with so many people involved, we made change.

Winning a Second Chance to Change Florida

Looking back now, over a year after passage, the campaign sometimes seems to have taken on mythological proportions, but more than anything, we owe our success to organizing. Although the campaign to pass voting-rights restoration in Florida grew to command tremendous resources, sophistication, and power, it didn't start that way. It started with elevating the voices of the most impacted people—returning citizens ourselves—and leveraging our stories to build a network of relationships and a narrative that brought disparate people together around a shared cause. The engagement of our campaign—people connecting with people—led Floridians to think of our issue through more than a partisan or racial lens.

Appreciating the challenges and opportunities in the Amendment 4 story requires understanding the larger context in which it was situated and the confluence of factors that influenced the strategy. It's one thing to transform your own life after struggling with addiction, homelessness, loss, and imprisonment. But figuring out how to persuade a majority of voters in Florida that such a transformation was possible sometimes felt insurmountable as a goal, especially in the early stages when there were virtually no resources, campaign experience, or even much encouragement, even from progressive allies. Rights restoration for returning citizens was the product of many years of work, but at the same time, it also aligned with our current cultural moment. We were able to have a much more open dialogue about racism, criminalization, and voter suppression than ever before.

The "unlikely movement" for rights restoration drew national and state groups into an unprecedented coalition with the power to finally upend over 150 years of Jim Crow and uplift 1.4 million disenfranchised voters. Once converted, many of the allies and "experts" who initially doubted that a citizen measure could succeed, became tremendous champions for the effort, contributing both legal support and significant resources toward organizing. Groups like the ACLU and the Alliance for Safety and Justice brought important credentials and voices to the campaign strategy. Faiz Shakir, the political director of the ACLU at the time, said, "We're challenging the notion that only certain people care about voting rights. Building a massive coalition across the ideological spectrum would send the most resounding message in a state like Florida. What you thought possible was totally wrong."[13]

And what *is* possible now? These legal advocacy groups have consistently pointed to the implications of the Florida victory for broader voting-rights advocacy and for criminal justice reform in the United States. In the aftermath of our victory, we have seen promising forms of this advancement, and refreshingly, returning citizens have been leading the charge. On the same night of the Amendment 4 victory, Voice of the Experience ("VOTE") successfully passed a constitutional amendment to eliminate a Jim Crow law that did not require a unanimous vote by a jury in order to convict someone of a felony offense. Our work on voting rights also influenced voting-rights work outside of Florida. In California, organizations like All of Us or None, A New Way of Life, and Initiate Justice worked with legal advocacy groups to successfully pass Proposition 17, which extended voting rights to returning citizens on parole or probation. In Louisiana and North Carolina, returning citizens were at the heart of litigation strategies that led to legal victories in each of these states for the expansion of voting rights to returning citizens. From 2018 to 2020, most of the major victories that expanded democracy were essentially led by directly impacted people. Throughout the country, people like me demonstrated that not only were we subject-matter experts as it pertained to criminal justice and voting rights, but we were also capable of being strategists and leaders of campaigns.

In the past, the voices of returning citizens were largely ignored by elected officials and policymakers in part because they were not viewed as a potential voting bloc. This was understandable because many of us were legally barred from voting, and a significant number of us wrongfully assumed that we could not vote and so did not register, and we did not present ourselves as a viable bloc. The future of our plight was largely left in the hands of policy "experts" who spoke on our behalf with or without our input or involvement, and elected officials who had little to no incentive to divert from their "tough on crime" stance. The recent victories are slowly changing that dynamic. Returning citizens are not only getting their voting rights restored, they are getting more involved in the policy discussions—no longer as a token, but now as powerbrokers. They are forming and leading coalitions, registering and turning out voters, and charting their own paths.

Lessons Learned from Second Chances Campaign

Amendment 4 has been called the largest expansion of voting rights since the passage of the Voting Rights Act in 1965.[14] In every way, it was a triumph for democracy both in the structure and process of the campaign and in the actual passage of the measure. While the victory takes on even greater significance in the context of the history of felon disenfranchisement and with consideration of the future opportunity to transform Florida by bringing more voices to the ballot box, we navigated many challenges to get here. And, as I'll discuss in the final section of this essay, we face similar challenges in the implementation of the victory if it is to have real impact on the lives of returning citizens. But first, let us take some useful lessons.

Directly impacted people provided an authentic voice to our campaign and drove the volunteer effort forward. They were at the heart of the Amendment 4 strategy. Post-victory, in the implementation phase, these returning citizens continued (and continue to this day) to play an equally critical role in ensuring that the strategy is accountable to the people it is intended to serve.

The Florida Rights Restoration Coalition led the Amendment 4 effort, but as the organization came to be increasingly prominent, it has become more organized and more structured. It is no longer a loose configuration of experts and allies. Today, the FRRC is a chapter-based membership organization consisting of formerly incarcerated people and their families from throughout the state. The FRRC also partners with an array of national and state allies and advocates to advance our mission to protect and implement Amendment 4 and also to connect the Amendment 4 victory to a longer-term agenda to advance policies that end mass incarceration, stop racial profiling and unfair policing, promote positive reentry policies, destigmatize returning citizens, and ensure improved public safety for all.

There is sometimes an inclination in truly transformational campaigns to romanticize strategy and downplay methodology. But in the case of the Second Chances campaign, there's been significant analysis of the deliberate choices that directly contributed to the campaign's success. That's because those same choices will be required in the subsequent phases of work to implement, defend, and protect the new law over the coming years. It can also help others who are engaged in efforts like these in their home states.

Authentic Leadership of Impacted People

The leadership by returning citizens was a lynchpin in the multidimensional campaign strategy. It helped preempt partisanship, define the narrative, manage relationships with allies and partners who might have otherwise coopted the campaign, and laid the groundwork for building a constituency beyond passage.

Political campaigns very commonly feature impacted individuals in press events, messaging, ads, and other roles that can lend credibility to the effort and help shape their narrative. Often, these people are tokenized, used as props, and excluded from meaningful decision-making when larger, more well-resourced groups come into a state to support a campaign. We had similar experiences with Amendment 4, but we leveraged our constituency and allies who were committed to our vision of returning citizen leadership, thus preventing us from being "bigfooted" by outside groups who ultimately were not long-term stakeholders in the Amendment 4 fight. Moreover, we benefited by having former felons who were themselves affected by this issue as the actual developers, drivers, and leaders of the strategy. Having agency, and even leadership, not just being the face of the campaign, is highly unusual and was sometimes controversial; some "experts" had other ideas about best ways to win.

The participation of returning citizens at every level ensured that the campaign stayed accountable to its constituency. No matter what other political or policy interests might lurk among partners, the increased participation of returning citizens in the electorate served as reminders that re-enfranchisement served everyone's interests, not just those of politicians who view these newly eligible voters as pawns in a larger game of power.

Anticipating and Preempting Opposition

News coverage of the Amendment 4 campaign noted time and again that there was very limited organized opposition to the ballot measure, certainly much less than anyone anticipated given the history of Florida. Limited opposition, however, was not an accident. It was an outcome accomplished by design. The campaign strategy from conception to implementation incorporated tactics designed to preempt and derail potential opposition, including opposition tactics that might leverage race, partisanship, or other polarizing elements to divide the electorate.

Among the most important steps to preempt potential opposition was the engagement of legal experts in drafting, vetting, and qualifying the ballot language. Lawyers from the NAACP, League of Women Voters, Advancement Project, ACLU, Brennan Center, and other allied groups played a critical role in helping forestall potential challenges from the Florida Supreme Court. Their work also informed the process we used to collect, validate, and submit signatures to qualify the measure at every step. Even in the implementation phase, a volunteer committee of many of the same lawyers continued to meet in preparation for potential state legislative challenges to the measure as well as to facilitate the county-by-county implementation of voter registration.

Nonpartisan Outreach and Bipartisan Consensus

The legal preparation to preempt opposition undergirded more public aspects of the campaign, as well, like narrative and field organizing. In both of these arenas, faith-based allies and outreach to returning citizens (no matter what their political affiliation) were critical features of our work. The campaign deliberately drove a values-based message that promoted consensus across constituencies and went beyond the specific issue of felony disenfranchisement. We stressed fairness, redemption, and hope.

The campaign didn't just "talk the talk" of consensus. It was actually built to reflect the very values it promoted. The bipartisan coalition included groups across the ideological spectrum, bringing together returning citizens from all over the state, from every race and ethnicity, and from all kinds of backgrounds. At the FRRC, our leadership included both women and men, Black and White returning citizens, and people from left- and right-leaning political backgrounds.

My close partner Neil was quoted in a news outlet as saying: "This is an issue that transcends the rural-urban-suburban divide. It transcends the partisan divide. And it really is something that impacts all communities and all walks of life."[15] The FRRC pushed the coalition to adhere to a balanced approach and to avoid the appearance of partisanship, even though it sometimes caused tension with the progressive Democratic groups whose political positions and language on other issues could be conflated with our specific agenda on Amendment 4. Progressive organizations might frame the initiative as "us against the conservatives" and use language like the "right to vote" (as opposed to voting being a privilege); these tend to create hard lines that prevent an opportunity for concession. We felt that it was important to create an environment that, at the minimum, allowed the opportunity for someone who instinctively opposes our efforts to be moved in our direction.

The campaign also received endorsements from a variety of organizations and public figures, which demonstrated its broad appeal. Among the endorsing organizations were the Florida Conference of Catholic Bishops, the National

Education Association, Our Revolution, and the Libertarian Party of Florida. High-profile leaders and celebrities also lent their support to the campaign, including the singer John Legend, Mark Holden (the chair of the Freedom Partners Chamber of Commerce), and an assortment of NBA and NFL athletes.

As it turns out, transcending partisanship proved to be a critical part of securing enough votes to pass the measure. Amendment 4 passed on November 6, 2018, with 64.5 percent of the vote. The statewide measure received more votes than any statewide candidate, including over one million votes from Republicans. The years of outreach, building a powerful grassroots groundswell of support, and statewide networks of relationships paid off on election day. But our task was then to see if they would continue to create capacity for implementation.

Old Habits Are Hard to Break

I've heard it said that nothing lasts forever, and that was the case with our campaign. Perhaps the most disappointing lesson of our experience—and one which is likely to be a fixture in any voting-rights activism done in our current climate—is that partisan posturing and litigation can tear apart a positive environment. In our case, it undermined the example we, to this day, continue to set for the rest of the country and other entities engaging in this work.

Importantly, we did not engage in scare tactics in order to get voter support for our constitutional amendment. We did not attack anyone or create an "enemy" to rally voters against. In fact, all we did was point to a broken system, and then appeal to people's sense of fairness while stoking feelings around forgiveness, restoration, and love. That's why when we saw over 5.1 million votes cast in support of our amendment, we knew they were votes not motivated by hate or fear. What we observed were votes based on love, forgiveness, and redemption. Election night demonstrated that love can in fact win the day, and that the people at the center of bringing such a diverse group of voters together were returning citizens; people who are traditionally viewed in a negative light or not given much thought. We showed the world that love is not only a force in personal relationships or times of tragedy, but also in movements to improve the lives of others and elections.

In addition to being able to move voters to act from love, our returning-citizen-led campaign created a dialogue around the expansion of democracy that was more about human decency and dignity, and less about partisanship. With pride, we were able to accomplish these feats in a political climate that was hyperpartisan and rife with divisive hate and fear. We ran a positive campaign that was the exception rather than the norm, and we had hopes of one day becoming the norm. Unfortunately, that would not be the case—even though positive, truthful, grassroots-led change is a standard that is (and should remain) the goal in democratic reform.

The infusion of politics and litigation quickly brought us back into the "business as usual" inertia. In Florida, we faced a Republican governor, speaker of the house, and senate president who insisted on getting involved in the implementation of Amendment 4, and on the other side were behemoth litigation/advocacy organizations. These huge and powerful forces always clash, bristling across sharp political lines, and we were right in the middle. What followed was a quick erosion of the world we had hoped to build. While we were still celebrating our amazing victory and the uniting of people, we couldn't avoid seeing trouble.

The Aftermath of the Campaign

Despite all we did to preempt challenges or opposition to our amendment; despite all of our attempts to keep our cause elevated about partisan politics, our predictions came true when Republicans in the state legislature took up Amendment 4 implementation in January, 2019—just two months after supermajority support from voters ensured its passage. Under the guise of "clarification," legislators introduced a bill that tried to alter the amendment's terms in ways that would have limited its impact.

The Florida legislature attempted to redefine key components of the amendment language. I likened this action to something that might happen to a (fictional) homeless family that is forced to live outside in the elements for several years. Every day, politicians walk past this family without ever offering assistance; without ever introducing and passing legislation to address the issues that keep them stuck on the street. Then one day, the community decides enough is enough; they come together and build the family a house.

But as soon as the house is finished, the politicians demand that only they, the legislators, can determine how the house is furnished. Thus the Florida legislature decided that only they could determine, for instance, what constituted "completion of sentence," and that they knew best which crimes still should disqualify a returning citizen from re-enfranchisement under the law. For instance, because returning citizens who commit sexual offenses and murder are excluded from Amendment 4, various legislators now sought to expand those definitions: the new terms would include prostitution under "sexual offenses" and include attempted murder and manslaughter under "murder."[16]

Additionally, the bill would also have mandated payment of court costs and fees to qualify for eligibility to vote. Amendment 4 already provided for completion of sentence, including restitution and fines associated with the conviction as part of eligibility; it did not, however, spell out those requirements in the language of the ballot measure. Therefore, in the Florida House of Representatives, there was an attempt to allow nonjudicial entities to expand the legal financial obligations beyond what was assessed at the time of sentencing. This meant that private entities like debt collection companies or other governmental agencies like the Florida Department of Corrections would be able to add more financial obligations such as cost of incarceration, or even outstanding medical fees, as a debt that must be settled before a person's sentence could be deemed complete.

The FRRC and its allies fought back against these attempts. We argued that the legislature could not expand the definitions of "murder" or "sexual offense" to include the additional charges, and that "completion of sentence" should not be broadly defined to include legal financial obligations that were not punitive in nature. At the core of our efforts was the desire to minimize the number of returning citizens that would be excluded from the immediate benefits of Amendment 4. Each of the legislature's potential changes had the potential to impact tens of thousands of returning citizens.

We were not naive enough to believe that every single returning citizen was going to have immediate access to democracy. Florida definitely didn't have the type of appetite for expanding democracy to returning citizens as broadly as Maine or Vermont had. We knew that in addition to the returning citizens impacted by the "carve-outs," there would be some who owed restitution, which meant not having immediate access to democracy.

The House bill passed in April, but thankfully, many of the provisions about the expanded definition of a completed sentence didn't make it into law, because they were merged with the more moderate Senate bill. The Senate bill focused instead on restitution, fines, and fees.[17] It would ultimately require returning citizens to pay all "court fees, fines and restitution" before they could vote. It also gave judges significant latitude to resolve outstanding charges, creating some opportunity for organizations like the FRRC to work with friendly judges, state attorneys, public defenders, and lawyers to expedite the process and qualify people to vote. However, the costs remain huge. In the last quarter of 2020, we raised over $23 million to assist with newly returning citizens' fines and fees, and this amount could help only 44,000 people; there are still 700,000 returning citizens in Florida who need this help. This is dire math, and an enormous number of people who continue to wait for their voices to be heard in our democracy.

Yet it's important to mark one's victories. On January 9, 2019, any amendment that passed during the previous election became officially a part of the state's constitution. So on that day, returning citizens across the state walked into the supervisor of election offices to register to vote. Throughout the state, they were greeted with confetti, balloons, and cheers. We were very intentional in touting January 9 as a day of love and celebration. We were intent on not letting the political pressure at the top dampen our spirits. We thought that January 9 was a great opportunity to do two things: amplify the message of love and become emissaries for democracy.

Every returning citizen who registered to vote was able to do so because love won the election. Each returning citizen had a family member or friend who loved them and believed in second chances, and because of that love, they voted yes on Amendment 4. Because of love, people like me now have a pathway to participating in democracy, and our first act was to register to vote.

It was not lost on us that as people who had lost our rights and fought hard to regain them, we now have a newfound appreciation for voting. It only made sense that we were the best emissaries to talk about how valuable that right to vote is, and how we honor it by becoming active participants in our democracy. We realized that we had an amazing opportunity to lead the charge to change the environment around voting; making voting something that people would aspire to do rather than regard as a chore. We wanted to make voting exciting again. Therefore, rather than harp on the negative political posturing, we chose to focus on people, and take whatever obstacle placed before us and turn it into opportunities to get even more people excited about democracy.

The excitement about participating in democracy was not just something we wanted to convey to returning citizens only. There were millions of people who were registered to vote but chose not to cast their ballot. There were also millions of people who were otherwise eligible to register to vote, but for some reason or another, had not done so. We wanted everyone to feel the passion for voting that we returning citizens had developed through losing our right to vote and then regaining it. Our democracy needs everyone to be involved in order for it to be vibrant. The people needed to be reminded of the passion we felt.

We also knew that *everyone* also included politicians. They needed to understand that one of the keys to a vibrant democracy, and one of their responsibilities as elected officials, was encouraging and facilitating total involvement in elections. Conveying that message had been one of the hopes that drove our work.

If we want a vision of what this energy looks like, we could do little better than looking to the offices of elections supervisors. When I walked into these places, I was overcome with an overwhelming urge not just to vote, but to know everything about elections. These supervisors were constantly active in the community. Whether it was at a local high school, or at one of many community events in which they partnered with other grassroots organizations, these supervisors were wholeheartedly encouraging people to register to vote. They were providing all sorts of information about voting that demystified the process. They were doing everything to make the act of voting enticing instead of intimidating. That's why I wasn't surprised when several of these supervisors actually rolled out the red carpet and had balloons to welcome returning citizens as they filled out their voter registrations. These supervisors understood that the lifeblood of our democracy is participation.

Yet we were not sure that the politicians in our state capital understood this; nor those in other halls of power, too. It seemed then as it does now that many politicians lean toward making it more difficult for people to vote, and even making it more difficult for everyday citizens to engage in the citizens' initiative process. These were the very same people who had the power to dilute the effectiveness of Amendment 4, so with the victory behind us, there was no getting around dealing with the statehouse and the courts. There was no getting around dealing with the "politics."

The FRRC worked across partisan lines to improve the bill as much as possible and secure these changes. Given that Republicans vastly outnumber Democrats in both chambers and legislation was sure to pass, our strategy was to leverage bipartisan influence to ensure the least harmful outcome. We were not only trying to minimize any potential damage. We were also trying to infuse the spirit of Amendment 4 into the legislative process. We had just shown the state that we could move a major issue without attacking each other or tearing each other down. We had just demonstrated that Republicans and Democrats were willing and capable of coming together to agree on giving second chances to people with felony convictions. If the "people" can do it, then why can't our elected legislators do it as well? We took this question and many others into our conversations with politicians throughout the capital. We carried the message of the 5.1 million voters who said yes to Amendment 4, hopeful that our message would not fall on deaf ears.

We did not fully understand what we were up against. We did not realize that we placed ourselves right at the center of an age-old battle between politics and litigation;

particularly between conservative politicians and progressive, litigation-based organizations, where the inevitable media engagement is a major driver of narrative.

Caught along with us were returning citizens who were taken on a rollercoaster ride of emotions, hope, and confusion. From the high of passing Amendment 4 to give 1.4 million returning citizens the right to vote, to the eventual low of the decision by the 11th Circuit Court of Appeals, which ruled that over 700,000 returning citizens would have to first pay any outstanding legal financial obligations before being able to register to vote, there was a series of ups and downs that dampened our message of excitement about democracy and made it more challenging to maintain the engagement of returning citizens.

The Unintended Consequences of Litigation on Organizing

Once Governor Rick DeSantis signed the bill into law that required returning citizens to satisfy their legal financial obligations prior to being able to register to vote, legal advocates led by the ACLU, the Brennan Center, and the Southern Poverty Law Center filed a suit challenging the legislation. While the move would earn some gains, those gains were limited, the process suffered because its separation from the grassroots, and media coverage instilled doubts in returning citizens.

The lawsuit argued that Amendment 4 did not require fines and fees to be settled as a condition of rights restoration. It was filed on behalf of (only) seventeen plaintiffs who could be affected by the new law because they could not afford to pay their financial obligations. The plaintiffs likened these legal financial obligations to a "poll tax," and they requested that the court enjoin the new law, preventing it from taking effect statewide until the legal challenge is fully resolved.

In October 2019, US District Judge Robert Hinkle issued a limited ruling that the state could not use these plaintiffs' financial hardship as a reason to deny them their vote. He did not wade into the bigger questions around the "completion of sentence" language, or of the constitutionality of Amendment 4 that has since come under scrutiny as that was a question for Florida courts, not a federal one. Instead, the judge issued an injunction that allowed the plaintiffs to register to vote and actually participate in elections.

Judge Hinkle's decision also declared that legislators created an "administrative nightmare" with their laws implementing Amendment 4 and suggested that they should take action to address it rather than depending on the court. The criticism was merited, as this administrative barrier is indeed huge: the state established that legal obligations had to be paid, but it created no clear or centralized way to track fines or fees. In other words, it was not clear how returning citizens were to find out how much they had to pay, nor how exactly they were to go about paying it. All this only added to the confusion among impacted people who may be deterred from trying to register because they mistakenly believe they owe money. In addition, many unpaid court fees and fines multiply with time, so paying these costs creates a huge burden for many people who are already struggling through the reentry process. Governor DeSantis could take action to fix the state's antiquated clemency process to expedite restoration of voting rights to returning citizens with outstanding fines or fees, yet the leadership insists the state can take no action until the case is fully resolved, which could take years.

There was no quick path toward resolution, not when Republican lawmakers saw themselves as benefitting from keeping the issue tied up in the courts, and thereby keeping returning citizens out of the ballot box. Yet voting advocates declared the initial decision a victory, even though it did not apply to any of the 700,000 returning citizens except the seventeen plaintiffs. And as a result, those hundreds of thousands of returning citizens did not vote in the critical 2020 elections.

In the wake of lawsuits following a victory like this there are often hidden landmines. For instance, in a departure from past work on Amendment 4, the litigation strategy had not been coordinated with the FRRC or other groups representing returning citizens. The FRRC was not a plaintiff in the lawsuit. The FRRC also refrained from commenting on the politics that were playing out between the

Florida GOP, the courts, and the legal advocacy groups who had taken up the cause.

Additionally, from the FRRC's perspective, the confusion and controversy created by the media coverage of these lawsuits had created what potentially could have become a greater impediment to progress than the actual legislation. Our challenge was magnified each day when voters—already disconnected from civic engagement—heard the persistent narrative that the Amendment 4 victory was moot because anyone with a fine or fee would not be able to vote or because the legislature circumvented the law with a new poll tax. Some experts had estimated that as many as 80 percent of returning citizens covered under Amendment 4 had some kind of financial obligation. Many would avoid registering to vote either because of their inability to pay or because of their uncertainty of whether they owed money and how much. Heightening their fear was the threat of prosecution because knowingly completing a voter registration card while being ineligible constitutes voter fraud—a crime in Florida.

In sum, it became clear that the legal tactics were absorbing much of the publicity around voting rights in Florida and increasingly reflecting the political polarization of the state. There was little consideration given to how the media coverage of these lawsuits would impact our efforts to reach returning citizens or to readily mobilize them to register to vote and engage in democracy. Meanwhile, legislators took advantage of the litigation to further polarize voters, while allowing our broken clemency system and problematic infrastructure limitations to persist.

So this is where things stand now: court challenges regarding this new law are slowly making their way through the system. We are hopeful that these challenges will be successful, but, in the meantime, many returning citizens are left in legal limbo. For now, our only alternative for helping these individuals is a county-by-county approach that enables smaller-scale activity based on local elected officials taking initiative to resolve fines and fees and register more people. This approach has some benefits, but also creates tremendous challenges with scale, resources, and impact in its aftermath.

Organizing in the Aftermath

Because it is so important that this work harnesses a vision of positivity, the FRRC tried our best to overcome the rising pessimism that was infiltrating the movement. We presented an alternative view of the impact of the legislation by pointing out that even though there were over 700,000 returning citizens with outstanding legal financial obligations, Amendment 4 created a pathway for 1.4 million returning citizens; which meant that there were approximately 600,000 of us who did not have outstanding legal financial obligations and could register to vote immediately.

In a state where presidential elections were decided by approximately 100,000 votes, adding so many new voters would mean that returning citizens could still be the deciding factor in local, state, and national elections.

Our message was very clear; in spite of the efforts to reduce the power of Amendment 4, the voices of returning citizens could not be completely silenced and there were more than enough of us to make a difference. We wanted to make sure that there was at least a glimmer of hope for returning citizens and for others who cared about democracy.

In addition to messaging, the FRRC designed several mechanisms to reengage returning citizens who are unable to register to vote because of remaining fines, fees, and restitution. While this program helps returning citizens ultimately be in a position to register to vote, it also provides another opportunity to engage with individuals who have been excluded from democracy, encouraging them to become involved with FRRC chapters and making it more likely that when they are able to register, they do so, and that when they are registered, they ultimately turn out to vote. Such a program could be a model to others. The initiative has three prongs:

1. Establish programs in judicial circuits in which there is an understanding among state attorneys, clerks of courts, public defenders, and judges to engage in an agreed-upon process that allows returning citizens to use the courts to

waive their legal financial obligations for the purpose of establishing voter eligibility.

2. Create a crowd-sourcing apparatus to raise funds to help returning citizens satisfy their legal financial obligations.

3. Use all social media tools along with a bus tour to locate and engage returning citizens who are otherwise eligible to register to vote, and to continue to create an excitement around civic engagement.

The dampening effect on voter registration and returning citizen engagement was an unintended consequence of the battle between politicians and legal advocates, but it did not completely defeat our efforts. That's why on election night in 2020, before the votes were even officially counted, the FRRC celebrated yet again. We threw a lavish party with music, food, drinks, and revelry. When asked why, our answer was simple. We felt that in spite of the final outcome of the election, we had already won.

We were celebrating the fact that over 100,000 returning citizens had an opportunity to vote in the most critical election this country has ever seen, and for many of them, it was their first time ever voting in a presidential election. We celebrated the fact that returning citizens in their fifties, sixties, and seventies voted for the first time in their lives. We celebrated the fact that when combined with family members in the households of returning citizens, almost 300,000 people voted, many of whom had no prior expectations of voting, or had thought themselves to be a part of our democracy. We celebrated the fact that the trend was showing the 2020 election to have the greatest number of voters in the history of our country, even in the midst of a pandemic. While there were many reasons people could have chosen to not vote, the overwhelming number of them did. I impressed on reporters that regardless of the eventual outcome of the election, people should be celebrating the expansion of our democracy; more first-time voters, more youth voters, and an impressive showing of returning citizens voting.

Not all returning citizens voted the same way. The reality is that just like there is a diversity of directly impacted people, there is a diversity of voters who supported our effort. While we, of course, hoped returning citizens would vote a certain way on our issues, what was most important was that they had the opportunity to vote at all—and they did.

The Amendment 4 campaign presented a challenge of overcoming seemingly insurmountable odds. But they were not so formidable as to scare us off. And because we were able to achieve success with the referendum, we see the new challenges ahead as opportunities for the people who are most directly affected to lead the charge. We know how to run a campaign that deemphasizes politics and rebuffs the political urge to partisanize our efforts. In short, we believe that we can do it again.

Conclusion

To close, I want to offer a coda to my story. Given all the work I'd done on Amendment 4, and the years of advocacy work that led to it, I thought that I fully understood the importance of our fight to ensure everyone had the right to vote. I had been an activist since 2006. I carried with me in-depth and personal experiences that informed my work. However, I was still not prepared for the experience of voting during the August 2020 primary election in Florida. It had been over *thirty years* since I last voted.

My earliest and only memory of voting was in 1985, the year I graduated high school. My voting precinct was at a church located three blocks from my home. I remember walking there to cast my ballot and feeling like I was engaged in "grownup" stuff. I don't recall having any pride or feelings of patriotism whatsoever. All I thought was that I was no longer a kid.

Now over three decades later, as I was walking up the path to the voting precinct, I was experiencing something entirely different. I couldn't help but feel that I was walking on hallowed ground. My mind went to all the blood that had been shed on American soil for people like me to have the right to vote. I thought about my ancestors who were beaten with clubs and mauled by dogs. I thought about the many ancestors of mine who were hung from trees and even burned alive in the attempt to keep people like me from experiencing the American Dream, to keep people like me from participating in our democracy. I even thought about the hundreds of volunteers who sacrificed blood, sweat, and tears to collect enough signatures to get Amendment 4 placed on the ballot, and sacrificed it all again to ensure that we garnered enough votes to meet the sixty-percent threshold. I also thought about the over 700,000 returning citizens in Florida who were unable to vote simply because they could not afford to pay their outstanding legal financial obligations.

All of these sacrifices were in the name of getting a chance to vote. I was indeed walking on hallowed ground.

I entered the precinct and was handed my ballot. I was directed to a small booth where I would be able to select the candidate of my choosing. As I started making my choices, memories of the various sacrifices made by others once again flooded my thoughts. I was conscious of how small the voting booth was and of my isolation at the time. I was engaging in a private act, an act no one was entitled to control. Whom I voted for was a secret between me and God. As the thoughts of this secrecy and the sacrifices to get here merged, I became aware that the act of voting may in fact be a sacred act; one that wrests the act of voting out of the destructive claws of partisanship and restores it back into its rightful place, mantled with our humanity. I realized that the act of voting was not a pledge to be Democrat or Republican, a conservative or progressive. My act of voting said two simple yet powerful words: it said, "I Am!"

I share this story because it is so easy for us to get caught up into the hyperpolitical nature or results of voting and lose sight of the humanity at its core. It is so easy for us to size someone up as a Democrat or Republican and feel driven to win—to advance our political or ideological agenda. Yet it's not right if we fail to see whom we are talking to. Whether it is the person whose dying wish was to be able to feel like they truly are a part of our society, or the person who wanted to vote so bad that every election in their city they would visit their local supervisor of elections office just to watch people vote, we can't afford to continuously miss the opportunity to recognize the humanity that lies at the heart of what we are doing, and to connect in that act with the humanity of each other. We cannot lose sight that our human connection should be more important than our political connection.

When efforts are centered around people rather than politics we have an amazing opportunity to bring people together and unite around the values that connect us. When we do so we are able to build a more robust democracy because more people feel welcomed into the process rather than dragged into it.

In our time, it has become so easy for us to politicize issues that are inherently not political. We've seen the polarization of something as simple as whether or not people deserve to not have poisonous water piped to their homes. I am, however, hopeful. We have all seen moments when politics and differences take a back seat to our humanity. Think about our reactions to natural disasters or other catastrophes. In the aftermath of a destructive hurricane, we all come together in the aid of our neighbors and even strangers. If we were to stop to assist a person who was just involved in a car accident, our first questions would not be, "Did you vote for Donald Trump?" or "What's your immigration status?" More than likely our first questions would be, "Are you okay?" and "How can I help?"

Our hyperdivisive climate demands a reset; a reset that gets us to a place where basic human rights, even our shared humanity itself, are not trumped by politics; a reset that gets us to a place where differences of opinions are not seen as a threat, but as a necessary element to vibrant discourse; a reset that gets us to a place where we understand that a vibrant democracy needs a steady infusion of votes, not a reduction in their number. The enfranchisement of returning citizens can be that reset button. The inclusion of such a large group of people from all walks of life, and all political persuasions, can infuse new life into our democracy—an infusion that's sorely needed.

Notes

1 Christopher Uggen, Ryan Larson, and Sarah Shannon, "6 Million Lost Voters: State-Level Estimates of Felony Disenfranchisement, 2016," The Sentencing Project, October 6, 2016, www.sentencing project.org/publications/6-million-lost-voters-state-level-estimates-felony-disenfranchisement-2016.

2 Nathalie Baptiste, "After Incarceration, What Next?" *The American Prospect*, January 26, 2016, prospect.org/civil-rights/incarceration-next.

3 Stacey Abrams, "Desmond Meade," *TIME 100 Most Influential People 2019*, time.com/collection/100-most-influential-people-2019/5567673/desmond-meade.

4 John Gramlich, "America's Incarceration Rate Is at a Two-Decade Low," Pew Research Center, May 2, 2018, www.pewresearch.org/fact-tank/2018/05/02/americas-incarceration-rate-is-at-a-two-decade-low.

5 Prison Policy Initiative, "State Profiles: Florida," www.prisonpolicy.org/profiles/FL.html.

6 "We Can Do Whatever We Want?' Not So Fast, Gov. Scott," *South Florida Sun-Sentinel*, March 28, 2018, www.sun-sentinel.com/opinion/editorials/fl-op-editorial-rick-scott-felon-voting-rights-20180328-story.html.

7 Ari Berman, "How the 2000 Election in Florida Led to a New Wave of Voter Disenfranchisement," *The Nation*, July 28, 2015, www.thenation.com/article/how-the-2000-election-in-florida-led-to-a-new-wave-of-voter-disenfranchisement.

8 *Johnson v. Bush*, 214 F. Supp 2d 1333 (SD Fla. 2002). Brennan Center for Justice, www.brennancenter.org/our-work/court-cases/johnson-v-bush.

9 "Jessica's Law," Wikipedia, accessed July 8, 2021, en.wikipedia.org/wiki/Jessica%27s_Law.

10 Florida Commission on Offender Review, "Rules of Executive Clemency," www.brennancenter.org/sites/default/files/analysis/FL%201%202007%20reforms.pdf.

11 Florida Division of Elections, Voting Restoration Amendment, 14-01, https://dos.elections.myflorida.com/initiatives/initdetail.asp?account=64388&seqnum=1.

12 Christopher Uggen, Sarah Shannon, and Jeff Manza, "State-Level Estimates of Felon Disenfranchisement in the United States, 2010," The Sentencing Project, July 2012, www.sentencingproject.org/publications/state-level-estimates-of-felon-disenfranchisement-in-the-united-states-2010.

13 Berman, Ari, "Inside the Unlikely Movement that Could Restore Voting Rights to 1.4 Million Floridians," *Mother Jones*, November/December 2018, https://www.motherjones.com/politics/2018/10/inside-the-unlikely-movement-that-could-restore-voting-rights-to-1-4-million-floridians.

14 Sam Levine, "The Biggest Voting Rights Win in Recent US History—and the Republicans Trying to Thwart It," *The Guardian*,

January 9, 2020, www.theguardian.com/us-news/2020/jan/09/florida-voting-rights-felons-amendement-4.

15 Tim Mak, "Over 1 Million Florida Felons Win Right to Vote with Amendment 4," WWNO New Orleans, November 7, 2018, www.wwno.org/2018-11-07/over-1-million-florida-felons-win-right-to-vote-with-amendment-4.

16 Florida CS/HB 7089: Voting Rights Restoration (2019), flsenate.gov/Session/Bill/2019/7089.

17 Florida CS/SB 7066: Election Administration (2019), www.flsenate.gov/Session/Bill/2019/7066.

About the Author

Desmond Meade, president and executive director of the Florida Rights Restoration Coalition (FRRC) and a returning citizen himself, played an instrumental role in the landslide 2018 Amendment 4 victory in Florida, which used the ballot box to restore voting rights to 1.4 million Floridians with a previous felony conviction. He is also chair of Floridians for a Fair Democracy, a graduate of Florida International University College of Law, one of *Time Magazine*'s 100 Most Influential People in the World for 2019, and Floridian and Central Floridian of 2019. His efforts in Florida present a compelling argument that creating access to democracy to those living on the fringes of society will create a more vibrant and robust democracy for all. He is the winner of the 2021 Brown Democracy Medal for his continuing work to restore voting rights, and connect Americans along shared social values.

CPSIA information can be obtained
at www.ICGtesting.com
Printed in the USA
LVHW111948081021
699943LV00009B/860